FROM BEAN TO BEAN PLANT

Anita Ganeri

www.raintreepublishers.co.uk
Visit our website to find out more information about Raintree books.

To order:
☎ Phone 0845 6044371
🖷 Fax +44 (0) 1865 312263
🖳 Email myorders@capstonepub.co.uk

Customers from outside the UK please telephone +44 1865 312262

First published in Great Britain by Heinemann Library, Halley Court, Jordan Hill, Oxford OX2 8EJ, part of Harcourt Education. Heinemann is a registered trademark of Harcourt Education Ltd.

Editorial: Nancy Dickmann and Sarah Chappelow
Design: Ron Kamen and edesign
Picture Research: Ruth Blair and Kay Altwegg
Production: Helen McCreath

Originated by Modern Age
Printed and bound in China by South China Printing Company

ISBN 978 0 431 05079 9
10 09 08 07 06
10 9 8 7 6 5 4 3 2 1

ISBN 978 0 431 05089 8
11 10
10 9 8 7 6 5 4 3 2

The British Library Cataloguing in Publication Data
Ganeri, Anita
From bean to bean plant. - (How living things grow)
571.8'2374
A full catalogue record for this book is available from the British Library.

Acknowledgements
The Publishers would like to thank the following for permission to reproduce the following photographs: Ardea pp. **4**, **11**, **12**, **17**, **29**; Corbis p. **7** (Patrick Johns); FLPA pp. **5**, **10**, **25**; GPL pp. **6** (John Swithinbank), **26** (Michael Howes); Harcourt Education pp. **18** (Trevor Clifford), **21** (Chris Honeywell), **22** (Chris Honeywell); Holt Studios pp. **8**, **9**, **14**, **15**, **23**, **24**, **27**, **29**; naturepl.com pp. **20**; Photolibrary.com p. **13**; Science Photo Library p. **16** (Moira C Smith).

Cover photograph of a bean pod reproduced with permission of Alamy Images/Carole Hallett.

Illustrations: Martin Sanders

Every effort has been made to contact copyright holders of any material reproduced in this book. Any omissions will be rectified in subsequent printings if notice is given to the publishers.

The paper used to print this book comes from sustainable resources.

Contents

Words written in bold, **like this**, are explained in the glossary.

Have you ever eaten beans?

A bean is a type of **seed**. It grows inside a case called a **pod.** The bean grows into a new bean plant. There are many kinds of beans.

These are some of the kinds of beans we cook and eat.

You are going to learn about broad beans. You will learn how a bean seed grows into a bean plant, makes new seeds and dies. This is the bean's life cycle.

These beans are broad beans.

Bean seeds

Bean **seeds** grow in the ground. Some beans fall out of **pods** from old bean plants. They stay in the ground over the winter. These seeds start to grow when the weather gets warmer.

Each seed can grow into a bean plant.

Farmers plant bean seeds in rows.

Farmers collect some bean seeds. They plant the seeds in their fields in spring. They water the beans to make them grow.

Sprouting seeds

The bean **seeds** start to grow in spring. In the bean are parts that will grow into a new plant.

The bean is a store of food for the new plant.

Rain makes the growing start.

The way the seeds start to grow is called **germination**. The seeds need sunlight and water to make them grow.

9

Roots and shoots

First, the **seed**'s hard case breaks open. Then a tiny **root** grows out of the seed. The root grows down into the soil.

The root helps to fix the plant in the soil.

The shoot is bent at first.
Then it straightens out.

The next part of the
plant to grow is a
tiny **shoot**. It grows
up through the soil
into the light. It has
tiny **leaf buds** at
the end.

11

Growing bigger

Over the next few weeks, the bean plant's **root** grows longer. It grows down, deep into the soil. Lots of little roots grow out from the main root.

*The roots soak up water and **nutrients** from the soil.*

The **shoot** also grows straighter and taller. It is now called a **stem**. The leaves at the end of the stem start to open.

The stem takes water and food around the plant. It also holds the plant up to the light.

What do the leaves do? 13

Green leaves

The bean plant's leaves open out and turn dark green. Like all living things, plants need food to live and grow. The leaves make this food.

The bean plants are growing well.

14

This picture shows how a plant makes its own food. The way a plant makes its food is called **photosynthesis**.

*The leaves take in gas (**carbon dioxide**) from the air.*

The gas and water are turned into food in the leaves.

The leaves take in sunlight.

*The **roots** suck up water and **nutrients** from the soil.*

Bean flowers

The bean **seed** has been growing for about six to eight weeks. Flowers are starting to grow. The flowers grow from small bumps on the **stem**. These bumps are called **flower buds**.

The flower buds start to grow in summer.

16

The flower buds grow all the way up the stem. They grow at the bottom of the leaves. The flowers have white petals with dark marks.

The flowers grow in big groups.

17

Insect visitors

Bees and other insects visit the bean flowers. You can see them buzzing around the bean plants.

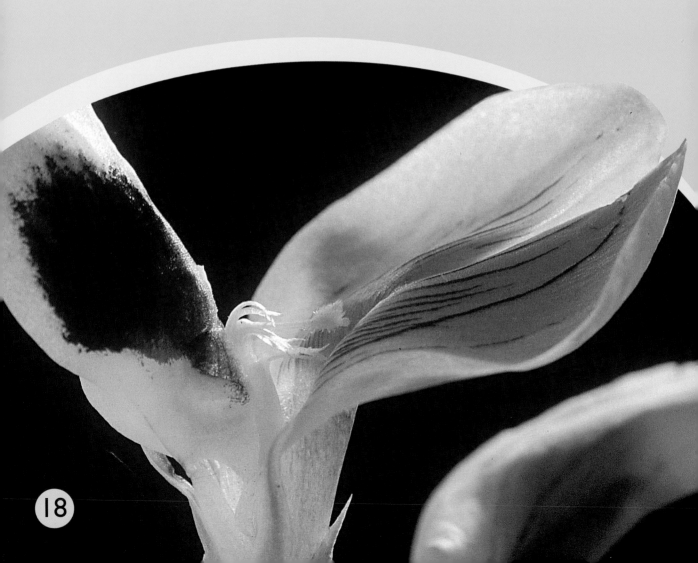

The bee has to crawl inside the flower to drink nectar.

The insects come to drink a sweet juice made by the flowers. The juice is called **nectar**. It is like an **energy** drink for insects!

19

Picking up pollen

The flowers also make a yellow dust called **pollen**. Some of the pollen sticks to the bee as it drinks **nectar**.

This bee is covered in pollen.

Then the bee flies to another flower to drink more nectar. There is still pollen on the insect. The pollen rubs off onto the new flower.

Bees can visit a lot of flowers in one day.

New bean seeds

The **pollen** from the insect joins with parts of the new flower. This is called **pollination**.

Lots of new bean seeds start to grow inside the flowers.

The new bean **seeds** are growing so the flower's job is done. The flower's petals droop and fall off. The flower dies.

Farmers know that when the flowers die, beans are on the way.

What is a bean **pod**?

Bean pods

The bean **seeds** grow in tough, thick cases. These cases are called **pods**. The pods keep the beans safe as they grow bigger.

At first the inside of a bean pod is soft and furry. The bean seed is small and pale.

Each bean seed is joined to the inside of the pod by a short **stalk**. The stalk brings food and water from the bean plant to the bean seed.

As the bean seeds grow bigger, the pods grow longer and thicker.

Splitting pods

In summer, people pick some of the bean **pods**. They take the juicy bean **seeds** out of the pods. Then they cook the beans. The beans are tasty to eat.

People keep some of the beans to plant next spring.

In autumn, the pods left on the bean plant start to turn black. Then the plant dies. Some of the pods split open and the beans fall to the ground.

The bean seeds will stay in the ground over winter. They will start to grow next spring. Then the bean's life cycle begins again.

Life cycle of a broad bean

10 Seeds fall to the ground.

1 Broad bean seed in the soil

2 **Seed** starts to grow in spring

9 Bean plant dies in autumn

3 First **root** and **shoot** grow

8 People pick beans to eat. They keep some beans to plant.

4 **Stem** grows taller and first leaves grow

7 New seeds grow in **pods**

6 Insects **pollinate** flowers

5 Flowers open in summer

Broad bean plant map

leaves

flowers

stem

roots

Broad bean pod map

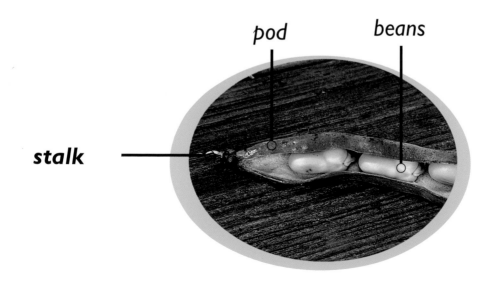

pod

beans

stalk

Glossary

carbon dioxide gas in the air

flower buds the start of flowers

energy strength to do activities

germination how a seed starts to grow into a plant

leaf buds the start of leaves

nectar sweet juice made in a flower

nutrients food living things need to grow

photosynthesis the way a plant makes its own food from sunlight, gas, and water

pod case that beans grow in

pollen yellow dust made in a flower

pollinate take pollen from one flower to another

pollination how pollen joins with parts of a flower to make new seeds

root part of a plant that grows into the ground

seed part of a plant that grows into a new plant

shoot new plant's first stem and leaves

stalk short stem

stem plant's tall stalk

More books to read

Life Cycle of a Broad Bean, Angela Royston (Heinemann Library, 1998)

Life Cycles: Broad Bean, Louise Spilsbury (Raintree, 2003)

Nature's Patterns: Plant Life Cycles, Anita Ganeri (Heinemann Library, 2005)

Websites to visit

Visit these websites to find out more exciting facts about life cycles:

http://www.bbc.co.uk/schools/scienceclips

http://www.ers.north-ayrshire.gov.uk/lifecycles

Disclaimer

All the internet addresses (URLs) given in this book were valid at the time of going to press. However, due to the dynamic nature of the internet, some addresses may have changed, or sites may have ceased to exist since publication. While the author and publishers regret any inconvenience this may cause readers, no responsibility for such changes can be accepted by either the author(s) or the publishers.

Index